# I KNEW

## The Struggle of Being on the Other Side

KUNHALI SYED

**ISBN**: 978-93-95266-18-5 (Paperback)

Any references to historical events, real people, or real places are used fictitiously. Names characters and places are product of the author's imagination.

Published by:  Beeja House

First Printing Edition 2023

**Author Email:** ksyed321@gmail.com

# Note from the author

*At a time when people were losing their heads over each other, when newspapers were plagued with stories of students committing suicide for matters as silly as losing a few marks, when youth would resort to murder for being turned down by their partner, when parents were scared to talk to their children, when tolerance was misconceived as weakness and arrogance as a virtue, is when I met the hero of this book.*

*He portrayed a sense of calm and spun a field of positive energy around him. He had a tale to tell. One that he narrated with a smile on his face. A tale so captivating that it had to be retold to the world.*

*Listening to him, I realized that my lack of capability in writing would not refrain me from conveying to the generation this story of valor. To tell the reader that the problems we have might seem a joke, were we to attempt to understand what goes around us.*

*Do not give up, for what you dream to achieve reposes ahead of your next attempt.*

# *Acknowledgement*

*If at all I am remembered, it will not be for my gratitude!*

*It is not that I am thankless, for I am raised well.*

*Taught to say 'please and thank you' by the nuns who schooled me, very early in life.*

*But the lessons my growing-up years taught me were more rigorous than those imparted by those living under vows of poverty, chastity, and obedience.*

*The years seem to have instilled in me a firm belief that man is bound by duty to assist fellow human beings when they progress along the journey of life.*

*Here's them who have gone beyond just duty to see my attempts materialize.*

*Cinin, my wife, who masters the subtle art of realizing when my mind gropes for words and creates space around me, regardless of where we might be, the dining table, my work desk or even while driving. She knows that her husband's mind operates in different ways in different situations & that it is extremely difficult to predict when it would experience a spark of creativity.*

*Alia and Abdullah, my children, both of whom could decipher the language of their mother's eyes.*

*All my friends on Facebook have been a great motivation, many a time finding more worth in my menial work than I ever realized.*

*Shabeera Seethi, who has been kind enough to volunteer insights into the plight of people with the rare medical condition of Intersex, where we grew up.*

*Apoorva Khare, who has carried out the mountainous task of editing this book.*

*To all of you, I remain indebted!*

***********

# Foreword

*Life is not meant to be a bed of roses; it never was, nor will it ever be!*

*From time immemorial, every cloud has been blessed with a silver lining as has every rain seen a shine.*

*The world will continue to be rocked by calamities, some man made, and others perpetrated by nature to bring mankind together as they stray far from the realms of humanity, many a time to disrupt lives of fellow human beings, fauna, or flora.*

*The same nature which lets us bask in pride and proclaim that we are out to save her when she possesses the ability to wipe mankind out at her will and fancy, will continue to exhibit signs of supremacy, signs which will be evident to those who have mastered the art of observing in silence.*

*The rich will have their problems, nor will the poor be spared. One will suffer for lack of means and the other for reasons numerous. Men will have their challenges, and so will women.*

*Mine were a little different. It had nothing to do with war nor flood. The challenges that men and women face seemed like something to desire compared to what I had at hand.*

*For I was born a fluke of nature! She had mocked the inhabitants of the world through me, they could not figure out if I was a boy or a girl!*

*This is a story of my fight against all odds, of deriving strength from failure, relying on the virtue of patience and of my undeterred faith in God Almighty.*

*The creator of man, woman, and me.*

***********

# 1981

# Jeddah 1981

## One

The tenth day of October was quite a normal one, winter used to set in early then, but Jeddah being a coastal town, was not prone to as dry a winter as was experienced in other parts of Saudi Arabia.

Somewhere back in history, 'Jidda', as the Hejazi pronounce it, was named 'Arous Al-Bahar,' which translates to 'Bride of the Red Sea'. 'Jaddah', is the Arabic word for 'grandmother'. Folklore has it that the Tomb of Eve, considered the grandmother of humanity, is located in Jeddah. The tomb is said to have been sealed with concrete, by religious authorities as people started praying at the site.

Being a Saturday, I chose the early hour of the day to leave my mother's womb and set foot into the world.

The delivery, I have heard my mother say, was as normal as the day, not any different from the other three my mother had prior to me being born. The eldest among us is my sister, followed by my brother the very next year. He enjoyed being the youngest child for eight years till my second sister was born, I was born in the year that followed. Exactly ten years after my mother's maiden delivery.

I am sure my dad would have reached the bank in time the day I was born, banks reopened on Saturdays after the weekend holidays, and it was important to report for work on the first working day of the week. Especially if it were to be around the tenth day of the month as that is when the expatriates used to get paid. Serpentine queues of people snaking right out of the bank, waiting patiently to send their earnings home, was a common sight. Many would take a day's leave to achieve the feat.

Paternity leave was unheard of in the early eighties, at least it wasn't heard of where I was born.

I have vague memories of my younger sister being born when I was three years old and quite clear ones of my youngest sister the following year. I was four years old then, and we were a family of six children, five girls, our brother who was planning to travel abroad for his studies, my mother who started falling ill frequently, and our father who used to keep us well-provided and ensured that our mother got the best medical attention.

Schooling for us girls was not an expensive affair as we all attended the local government school, the same was the case for my brother too for his primary and secondary education; not until he travelled to Russia did his education start weighing on the family.

I was a very shy kid at school and was terrified of my first teacher. I dreaded the thought of having to roam around the school with a placard reading 'I am stupid' pinned on my back! This is what the teacher used to do if we got our schoolwork wrong. I flunked my 1st std exams and had to repeat the year. Thankfully, my father moved me to a different school and took upon him the responsibility of teaching me to read. The teacher at my new school was a sensible lady and I started to do exceedingly well in class. I ended up collecting not less than fifteen riyals every day from my father as it was agreed that he would pay me 1 riyal for every star I was awarded in class. I remember waiting for him to arrive from the office, books in hand, making him count the stars and collecting the money even before he could change his clothes.

We lived a normal life like any other middle-class family, but all of us learnt very early in life not to disclose everything for the fear of our mother falling sick, we learnt never to talk twice about how we felt, not even between us, for if it was not heard the first time, it never would be. My dear mother was diagnosed with schizophrenia, and we were made wise to the fact that the slightest pressure on her brain would result in her getting bedridden. Back then the disorder was considered more the work of spirits than having to do with one's physical or mental condition.

Our lives revolved around making all the sacrifices we could to ensure that we get to see our mother smiling when we return home from school! We carried a prayer on our lips always! The first drops of rain that arrived to soak the parched earth made me lift my arms heaven wards and ask God Almighty to cure my mother of her illness, to make her hug me as every other mother did her child. She heard voices and remained paranoid.

But again, we trusted more in getting her cured through *sheikhs* even though we sought for her the best medical treatment. The nature of celebrating sorrows is embedded in our family. We remained thankful that the matter was not worse and happily reconciled to our lot. We knew very well that there was less than a percent chance of a person being diagnosed with a mental disorder of this magnitude, but we were still thankful that our mother was with us.

My father tried to fill in the void left by our mother when she remained in bed. Time being limited, as he worked at the bank, he tried to achieve with money what we missed in attention. I don't think he had any friends. He used to come home straight from the office and spend whatever time he had, in our company. We played cards for hours together, so engrossed in the game that we played in silence till we went to bed. The eldest of our sisters started to assume a motherly role, and we four sisters bunched up together. We had three cousins of the same age who used to join us often in our girlie games. We learnt to share and fend for each other as we grew up. We became extremely good at keeping our secrets too.

I was the naughtiest of the lot, marks of which I still carry. You would notice that my left hand is bent like a bow because of being fixed rather hastily when it was fractured. The ayurvedic doctor who attended to the fracture was apparently not very experienced and managed to somehow bind the fracture together. We didn't bother much about a bent arm at home, if I could use my arm, it was all fine.

I made frequent trips to the sweetshop close by, if not to buy sweetmeat, then to ride on the merry-go-round for which the shopkeeper charged one Riyal per ride!

These journeys to the sweetshop led to an incident that would help you understand the nature of my father, and us four girls better. Seeing us sneaking out of the house ever so often, our father decided to check what we were unto. He followed us to the shop. Seeing us pay one Riyal each for the ride on the merry-go-round, he bought the entire thing and installed it on the terrace for us to take as many rides as we wanted to. The ride had four seats, out of which, one didn't have a hand rest, my elder sister volunteered to take the broken seat, that explains her, she loved to play the role of the eldest amongst us four, ready to sacrifice for our happiness, she seemed to be growing too fast, trying to ensure we didn't miss our mother's care and grooming. The one younger to me was the smartest and she would read whatever she could lay her hands on. She is the one in the family who had received the traits of my father. We had a good collection of books, which, apart from every book written by Agatha Christy and translated into Arabic, included *Encyclopaedia Britannica*. I wanted to open the ball bearings on the pedestal and check what made it go around so smoothly with so little effort, I was more interested in its mechanics than riding on it. The youngest amongst us would join me in pushing the ride around before we jumped into our seats. There was a fax machine at home too, the only one in the vicinity. My father used to fax us outlines of pictures from his office which we were to colour with crayons by the time he returned home. These were the games we used to play. It was a happy home, but we lived like cattle behind our veils. Our dreams were limited to owning Nintendo, Sony play station or Atari games. We wrote a letter to our brother listing down our dreams, a Sony play station topped the list and he brought home one for us! Such was our life, our dreams so simple that they could easily materialise.  I took a liking to cricket and started playing the game. No one ever stopped us from playing whatever games we decided to play. Our father didn't stop us from doing anything we wanted to do.

When the Gulf war broke, our games changed. We had blackened out our windows and used to enjoy the blackout drills. The air raid sirens used to send us scurrying to the ground floor. We had stored food, enough for weeks. When I think back about it now, it was more of fun and excitement to us kids.

I recollect the whole family leaving for Qatar for my cousin's wedding. I had sprained my leg and enjoyed being pushed around in a wheelchair. We stayed for a week in Qatar and were quite excited about living in a farmhouse. It was a big house and the place had horses, camels, and cattle. The experience was quite enriching and for the first time in my life, I realised people lived in places other than in flats and apartments.

My brother, I recall, being quite busy, he travelled to Australia when he was fifteen. He was supposed to be going abroad for higher education, but the actual purpose was just to learn English. Mastering the Queen's language was considered a major milestone in one's education then, when a certain percentage of the population was unaware of the fact that there were other means of communication than speaking in Arabic! He returned after 6 months but his English wasn't any better. He learnt to drive a car quite early, as every kid in the country did. He was involved in a traffic accident the following year which resulted in the death of a senior citizen. According to the rules of the country he would have to end up in jail for a good part of his life, the situation at home was grim, but he was lucky to have been pardoned by the old man's relatives. Loss of life in road accidents is considered very grave in the country and there are stories of people having had to spend their entire life behind bars. If ignorance is found to be the reason behind the accident, the state serves very stern punishment.

Thankfully, my brother was released after spending one month in jail, he returned home quite withdrawn into himself. He became quite religious too.

My father was the second person in the country to undergo pancreas transplant surgery, the first one was successful, but my father's transplant wasn't, it was a failed surgery, and my father was destined to be on insulin for the rest of his life. With the surgery, the winds of despair started blowing through our otherwise happy home.

I was eight years then, but I could see the desperate race of a man, who was trying to settle his family, in my father. He was in a hurry to get his eldest daughter married, there was a quick change of plans, and it was decided that she would be married to her first cousin, and they would live on a floor in the building we lived in. The building belonged to us.

My sister got married, and the first baby arrived the very next year, a healthy girl. Like my father, my brother-in-law also worked in the bank.

The following year marked the birth of her second daughter, Jamila, and when she was pregnant for the third time with her son, in the third year of the marriage, is when the family noticed something odd with Jamila. I was grown-up enough to feel the tension mount in the house, hushed conversations, prayers, and tears being wiped. I saw the fighter in my sister then! Her regular trips to the hospital, fighting against every odd. The hospital visits had nothing to do with her being pregnant, for maternity was a very casual affair in our house and among our relatives. Neither I nor my three sisters knew what the tension was all about.

We felt the strain, my father looked concerned, my mother remained on her bed most of the day, and my sister's trips to the hospital became an everyday affair.

One day, they took Jamila to the hospital, and we wondered why they had dressed her up as a boy!  We were clueless about what was happening, until after a week, when they brought her back as a boy, and told us that we should call him Jamil. We destroyed every picture we had of him dressed as a girl.

1991

# 1991

# Two

The Lebanese pound tumbled to 1,838 per dollar, rendering it unworthy of the paper it was printed on! On its unconstrained journey downhill, it wiped out my father's savings too.

A recent study published by a renowned business school in Jeddah states that every third quick service restaurant, especially the gourmet burger joint and coffee shops, which we see springing up in prime localities, is ventured by students who have returned from western countries without having completed their education, for which they were sent there by their parents.

My brother had achieved this feat way back in 1990 itself, he had realised quite early that one had to put in as much effort as one did in Saudi to pass the exams! Having returned from Russia without completing his education, he had opted to try his luck in the share market. Even then he knew that building a brand would be a colossal task and opted for an easier route to earn. He invested all my father's savings in Lebanese companies.

I have never seen my father get agitated, or lose his cool. The closest he got to losing his temper was with me, when I was found playing with his medicine vials. I liked the vials as they came with a syringe handle, they were SAR 2000 apiece and he had to take one every week. I picked half a dozen from where it was kept and was found playing with them. He pulled his belt out but calmed down when he saw the tears in my eyes.

My father took the loss in investment without any fuss. He had the faith to start all over again, but the uncertainty arising from his health condition was quite evident for anyone to read.

The wind of despair continued to blow; the drizzle turned into a downpour! My father lost his job in 1994. The country aimed to employ its nationals by replacing expatriates from important positions in government and semi-government institutions. The move left many expatriates in very good positions, jobless.

My father decided to get into business. Everyone leaving the country carried electronic gadgets, not only those who were going for good but those who were returning home on vacations also purchased televisions, radios, music systems or at least a torch to carry home. A shop selling electronic gadgets seemed the most ideal choice. It took less than three months for us to start reasoning why no one wanted to buy from our shop and how our competitors could sell at prices below what we paid to purchase! The new venture failed to generate any revenue; not even enough to pay the shop rent.

For the first time, we went through the dire situation of not having enough money in the house to have food on the table and I realised my helplessness in making it better. There was despair in the house, a sense of doom, the walls of the house started echoing money, or the lack of it rather. My father used to have cornflakes for breakfast, which suddenly seemed like a luxury. It became unaffordable and we resorted to having eggs with *khubz* (flatbread). We were a proud family, we prayed, we went to sleep hungry but never complained, nor did we borrow. I used to share my father's cornflakes in the good days. I did not want to exhaust the little that was remaining, I recall crushing just one flake, sprinkling it over my cup of milk, and having it!

I was turning ten when I first experienced sexual stimulation. It was raining and all my friends were playing in the rain during the mid-day recess. The practice of coeducation was unknown in Saudi and the school we went to had only girls. I sat in one corner watching the girls drench themselves, we were all reaching puberty and the girls had breasts in different stages of development, showing through wet clothes. I was fascinated, but the fascination was laced with anxiety and a sense of guilt. I tried to fend off all lewd thoughts that entered my mind but gave in to the comfort of being aroused and watched the girls, with a sense of peace descending on me! I begged to be forgiven when I offered prayers, but somewhere in the corner of my mind lurked a feeling that was new to me, I kept recalling the sight of the pink areola and the firm forming nipple jutting out against the drenched white uniform shirts, refusing to be constrained by it.

One other matter, the thought of which amuses me now, was my yearning to wear trousers. I longed to wear trousers and fantasised about going out in one, but again, religion had such influence on me that I felt guilty about being tempted to do what decent God-fearing girls were not supposed to do! Dress like boys! I called a truce between my mind and heart by wearing my brother's trousers beneath the *abhaya* and going to my uncle's house to meet my cousins. Yet, the guilt caused a knot in my throat, one which I could neither swallow nor spit. I lost sleep over it at night but the thought of having worn a trouser made me feel ecstatic. My father had no objection to whatever we girls wanted to do but we had built a shield of religion around us, restraining ourselves from what we believed was forbidden for girls. This, I now realize, was one reason that I didn't probe further into my genital deformation too. We strictly lived within the parameters we had drawn for ourselves with our father playing the role of provider. He would provide whatever we required, thus keeping us busy all the time. I do not know if that was his way of keeping me protected from the world outside.

My mother continued to remain bedridden, we tried our level best not to let her know, nor to be affected by the financial situation, we ensured that her medical care was prioritised over our food. We took turns nursing her and did our level best to carry a smile when we entered her room. She heard voices and remained quite disturbed and paranoid during the schizophrenia attacks.

I realise now, that this was the pivotal period of my life, I dropped out of school and decided to help my father. With the electronic shop going from bad to worse, he started doing a data entry job for students and teachers at the university. While he had considerable speed in typing English, he was helpless with Arabic. I took over the Arabic part and became quite efficient in no time. I became good at data entry and my elder sister did the formatting. She became good at graphics, and all three of us started working in tandem. Our turnaround time was quite fast and the quality of our work was very high, we started getting flooded with work.

The work helped not only in easing our financial strain, but it changed my perspective. Most of the data entry I did was related to research material, some of it was thesis for submission by students and the others research results by professors. One day I would work on research relating to pain, on the other day on plastic, and on the third, on addictive behaviours. I gained immense knowledge during that time as I used to try and understand what I was working on. Unlike today, the internet was just being made available to households, and the data available on the net was only a fraction of what it currently is. I got to sift through a lot of valuable information, and I took a liking to organise it in my mind while I typed the projects neatly.

My brother was doing odd jobs but was not able to assist in reversing the financial condition at home.

My probing nature made me shift my interest from dismantling and reassembling remote control cars to taking apart the computer at home. The insides of a computer intrigued me, I vividly recall an incident when I had gone to sleep with the computer dismantled and the motherboard not being able to be fixed back into the slot. My father saw the mess and woke me up to remind me that he reads the news on the internet at daybreak and wished to do so the next morning too. I didn't sleep that night to ensure that the computer could connect to the net and my father could read the news even though some of the parts had to be held together with my ribbon. As a reward, he gifted me with a book on computer hardware, which I put to good use and became extremely good at repairing computers. I could troubleshoot all hardware and software issues.

The following year, my father sold off the electronic shop, my brother sold his car, and we opened a shop near the university to do what we did at home in a more organised manner, my skills in using and repairing computers extended to doing so with flatbed scanners and DVD writers which were new to the market then.

However hard the times were, I realised that I am blessed with a photographic mind. I could effortlessly recall circuit diagrams, use any new computer gadget, set them up, repair them, and not only could I speak

Arabic like a native, but I could convince anyone of what I wanted to convey. I was compellingly beautiful too, the most beautiful amongst us sisters. While we rarely mingled with men, I was quite used to females staring at me!

It is the law of nature that the opposite sex attracts, but it felt strange to have my friends wanting to be close to me! Stranger still when it started to dawn on me that there was something in me that had girls swarming around me. In a society where genders never mingled, girls of my age fought for my attention. I should admit that I started enjoying it. I basked in the sunlight and felt exalted when I noticed girls competing to be with me. There was this girl who used to bring flowers for me regularly, laugh at whatever I would say and not like it when some other girl was seen with me. Along with all of what was happening, I started to realise that my interests weighed more towards what men did.

Motor vehicle was completely a man thing, females were not allowed to drive. I yearned to drive, and I was quite sure that I would be able to master driving in very little time, I was quite confident that I would be able to figure out what goes under the hood too. My confidence was not limited to understanding the working of a car, I had no doubt that if given a chance I would do exceedingly well in whatever I chose to do to earn a living. But then, chances were very limited, if any, for the fairer sex then.

I remained quite busy for a girl of sixteen, helping my father at his shop, and handling research material. I even started pointing out mistakes in the submissions to the research students at the university. I became quite famous in the corridors of the university, among the students and the professors too.

The year 1997 saw the advent of the internet; I was successful in convincing my father that the internet was required at home. He was reluctant at first, thinking of the negative impacts it could have on a house full of young women. It didn't take me more than a week to change his thought process and ensure that our household was connected.

At home, I started noticing a change in my sibling's behaviour towards me, I could see them huddled together discussing in low tones. They stopped the moment they saw me and disappeared to different corners of the house.

It reminded me of the times when Jamila was born. Of a time when everyone seemed to be weighed down with despair, when frown replaced the smile on every face.

No one had to tell me that there was something abnormal with me, it was quite evident that there was something very wrong. Girls of my age had started to change, not only were they growing taller and gaining weight, but their hips were also getting wider and their bosoms fuller. I realised that I was not growing breasts, my upper lip started sprouting fine hair and above all, I had not had my menstrual periods too!

The thought of being aroused while watching girls of my age returned with a sense of guilt and fear. It invaded my entire body, travelled through my nervous system, making me weak and scared. I could feel it right from the middle of my head to the tip of my toe. I felt exhausted when alone, and strange when in the company of my sisters, as I could sense them eyeing me covertly. To add to my misery, it dawned on me that whatever conversations my friends were having about boys did very little to fascinate me.

I found myself lost in thought, trying to recollect incidences right from when I was a toddler when I was attracted more towards girls than boys.

It felt like being on a roller-coaster ride and realising that the harness had snapped!

# 1998

# *1998*

# *Three*

If confusion could kill, I would not have survived the year!

The ordeal of trips to the hospital started, and the visits were quite a tedious affair. The doctor had a busy schedule and the wait for consultation was long and tiring. It was my eldest sister and my mother who took me to the hospital, though unwell, my mother made it a point to accompany us, and my father, not to. After being inspected, the doctor used to brief my mother and sister, not a word was spoken in front of me. Uncertainty started building, making it torturous, but the way we were brought up refrained me from asking, and the way the society was, saw no reason to reveal to me what I was ailing from!

It would seem insane, but the prospect of having cancer came as a relief to me. Such was the state of my mind. The thought that cancer could be curable rekindled some hope of returning to normalcy and I was tempted to ascribe all that I was going through to something as simple as cancer! To think of the worst, to know what I was dying of would bring me a lot of relief than groping in uncertainty, trying to figure out why everyone in the house behaved the way they did when they saw me.

I tried keeping myself busy tending to my nephew who was just a few months old. With my sister remaining busy and me seeking distraction, the boy fell into my lap naturally. I fed him, cleaned him, played with him, and spoiled him too.

Not only was the year a confusing one, it was merciless too. My father lost two of his brothers, one to heart failure and the other followed in a weeks' time from a broken heart. They were quite close to each other and my father to both. The loss weighed heavily on my father, it was quite visible and started reflecting on his health. His eyesight started deteriorating and his diabetes became worse. I later realized that my state of affairs would have bothered him the most. I used to watch him visit me in bed when I went to sleep, feeling my forehead thinking that I was asleep. I would watch his lips shiver in prayers and his misty eyes close in sorrow, like that of an eagle's, watching her eaglet struggle in pain.

During a visit to the hospital, I was asked to prepare for medical surgery. Again, I witnessed hushed-up discussions in the house, but topics swiftly changed when I was spotted. It felt odd when one saw a group of people discussing the weather in subdued voices and grim expressions! I saw my brother signing the consent on the yellow hospital documents. To date, it runs a shiver through me when I recall the doctor asking me, "Are you sure that you are a girl?" I was dumbfounded and even looked over my shoulders, not sure if the question was addressed to me! "Sure," I murmured, not knowing that I had condemned myself to doom by saying so.

I underwent medical surgery in October. I recall friends and relatives visiting me in the hospital and thanking God for his mercy in curing me of cancer.

A thought kept haunting me when I surfaced after the surgery, I was not sure if it was hallucination. Just before I was carted in into the theatre, I heard the nurse telling my mother that we would come to know my gender after the ultrasound scan, which I was about to go through. I saw my mother lose her calm and ask the nurse to shut up. All through the days in the hospital, I tried to figure out if it was a dream, the sight of the same nurse in flesh and blood made me realise otherwise.

When I returned home a week after the surgery, my father was at home. He had tears in his eyes when he saw me, he laid his hand on my head and told me that I will surely be rewarded for my patience. I was not sure what he meant but started losing hope that the surgery I had gone through would help clear the uncertainty that was grinding me down.

A week after the surgery, I started bleeding and was rushed to the hospital. When they were preparing me for inspection, I asked the nurse if this could be my menstrual period. Her response ran shivers through my body. "You do not have a uterus!" is what she said.

These strings of events saw me slipping from bad to worse-

The bleeding had resulted from the ripping-open of a suture and was taken care of. A six-inch surgical mark under my belly button, the removal of swelling from beneath my private part, which I later realised was scrotum and one red pill to be consumed every day was all that remained.

I tried to reconcile by thinking that it could be cancer of the uterus that I had suffered from. My friends and neighbours who visited me shared the same thought. I thanked God that I had been saved from cancer but couldn't gather the courage to seek answers to the questions I had, from people at home.

I was more confused than ever! I resorted to seeking answers from God Almighty.

I became very religious and took up learning the Holy book very earnestly. This brought peace to my mind, the storm in me started to calm down, my mind didn't race as it did and I could see rays of hope, possibilities of being able to return to normalcy. I pooled my sisters also along with me, and we gave up watching television and went to the extent of tearing up all the family photographs. With the solace it brought, I started focusing only on religion and suppressing all other thoughts and emotions. It could have been my plight that made me so desperate to flee from reality, the hormone imbalances and medication had started to shatter me.

My father disapproved of our change, he tried to tell us that religion did not require us to sacrifice the way we did, but he could not force us, as we all looked very determined and pleased with the new ways we had adopted. It wasn't in him to stop us from anything we were doing, he would hint his disapproval of matters that didn't appeal to him but would never enforce his opinion or snatch away whatever little freedom was allowed for us girls.

My brother got employed at the bank, with him working at the bank, the financial conditions at home improved. The moment he started paying the bills he started exercising control over family matters. It went unnoticed till we lost our father, but for me, it became a matter to deal with in the later years. His thoughts had very little semblance with those of our father and with every day progressing he was growing apart from every member of the house.

My father died on the 18th of April 2003. He died of heart failure. Having slipped into a coma on the way to the hospital, he remained bedridden for three days. I recall receiving a phone call from the hospital and a cold voice informing me that my father was dead and that we could collect the body from the hospital! The line went dead, and so did something inside me. I did not cry for two days; I was more worried about my mother and did not want her to break down beyond repair. My father loved and cared for my mother, the last words he uttered before slipping into coma were to take care of our mother. Not until my aunty came home after two days, did I cry, and then, I wept my tears dry. Losing my father, I came very close to losing hope, I had to remain on my prayer mat to hold on, not to give up, and to continue to live to discover what lay on the other side of life. We grieved the loss of our father, I found solace in praying for him, it somehow made me miss him less. I prayed for him in the early hours of the day and late into the night after the Isha prayers.

My brother got married in the month of September the same year and started living in the family house. He chose a bride from Syria who settled in our house very comfortably as we all could speak Arabic perfectly well. My youngest sister got married in 2004 and went to live with her husband. She got married to a Saudi and settled down well at her in-law's, just like my brother's bride did at our place.

One occupation that was allowed for a girl in Saudi, then, was that of a teacher, and I chose to teach. My elder sister was teaching in a college, and I also took up a teaching job. I was invited to give classes on computer hardware by an institute that offered a diploma in computer science to students. I spent nights trying to understand what needed to be taught and within a very short period became the most sought-after teacher by the students in the institute. Computer science became the most interesting subject for most of the students, and I kept my classes to the point. I was obliged to remain to the point as my expertise was limited to the practical repairing of the computer with very shallow knowledge of the hypothesis. I found a reason for my living and discovered my skill in teaching. I thoroughly enjoyed my work but left the job within a year. It was none of my business, but I couldn't agree with how the institute had terminated the services of one of the employees. Apart from teaching, I discovered my organising skills, having made all the employees resign in protest. The management tried to convince me with a hike in pay, but it never was in my nature to retract on commitments.

I lost the job, but the event marked the start of a great relationship. I met Amna who was the receptionist at the institute. A thin and frail girl to whom I took an instant liking, I used to carry chocolates for her and enjoyed having them with her in between classes.

I decided to pursue my education, found another friend who had dropped out of school, and we jointly resumed our studies.

In the year 2007, my younger sister got married and the one elder to me got married in 2008.

Life seemed to shift gears and days gathered pace, I got busy and remained quite popular amongst my friends. I was invited to every party within our group, be it weddings or get-togethers during the weekends. It was quite a trend then, that women got together at the weekends, renting chalets by the sea and partying through the night. I had a party to attend every week.

I was not fully in control of myself, the hormones I was prescribed by the doctor had a role to play. They worked on me physically as much as they did on my emotions. I started realizing that I had in me something that attracted both females and males. I started enjoying the attention till a girl who was my neighbour tried slitting her wrist because I didn't attend to her phone call! I had a group of friends who all tried to huddle close to me. Somewhere around the time, I got in touch with a boy online. We shared the same interest in computers and discussed for hours the advancement of technology. He used to attend all the technology exhibitions, collect brochures, and leave them on my doorstep for me to read. In the course of our friendship, he introduced me to his sister, to whom I took a liking. He intended to reach me through his sister, but it so happened that I got to her through him!

The times were too good to last and the year that followed seemed to demand a toll on the good times I had had! I was left alone at home with my mother, my brother, and his family. I spent time babysitting my nephew, life started becoming difficult with my brother imposing restrictions on me and I continued taking my tablets. It could have been inactivity that started distorting my mind again. No person who has not been through it will ever understand how drugs and hormones can influence a human body and mind. You will feel your heart being torn apart and fail to understand why. You will pray that your mind stops thinking for a split second; more so, you will bang your head on a solid surface to stop your mind from racing just to realize that your heart has joined your mind and is racing faster! To top it all, the feeling of guilt, guilt for the way you have been thinking, for not being in control of your thoughts and the feelings these thoughts are leading into.

As if the hurdle of the day did not suffice, dreams started disturbing me at night. I had the first such dream where I dreamt of matters related to the Holy book, the dream disturbed me a lot and I contacted a scholar who has done her doctorate in Islamic studies. I spoke to her of my dream, she was shocked, found my dream to be absurd and it took some time for her to decipher it. She called me back to say that my dream could only mean the birth or arrival of a boy. It did not make much sense to me then and helped further disturb my confused brain. I was scared that I was losing my senses and would have to suffer again what I had experienced earlier.

I started having differences of opinion with my brother. We found it difficult to agree on any matter. I sensed intolerance in him, he attempted to subjugate me. Obstinacy and pride ran in the family, we could disconnect and maintain silence for days and weeks together. The trait, as I said, ran in the family and it was deep-rooted. I wanted to go to college and my brother refused. He started putting restrictions on my movement, I was not allowed to go out of the house, visiting my sister a few buildings away became a 'once in a week' affair. I had friends visiting me at home, and they made sure to arrive after my brother had left for work and to leave before he returned.

I remained indoors but depicted my disagreement by getting a projector and turning my room into a theatre. I gathered all my friends to watch *Slumdog Millionaire*. I was confused, I was scared, but I still had the fight in me. The theatre did not last for long as my brother broke the projector during one of the discussions we were having.

I do not know whether it was the surgery that I had undergone or the tablets that I was having, or both, that smoothened my skin and softened my voice. All traces of facial hair disappeared, and I had blossomed into a woman any man would desire.

I got my first marriage proposal in 2009. The suitor was a rich guy who owned a laterite block factory. We got engaged but the marriage could not go through as he failed to obtain government approval to marry an expatriate. The law required getting clearance from a lot of government bodies for a Saudi national to marry an expatriate. A process that is known to be long, tedious, and cumbersome.

The second proposal was from the owner of a few dozen petrol pumps, three wives and twenty children. He was fed up with the kids and wanted to get married to someone incapable of having children. I fit the bill for him, but I declined.

The third was from a high-ranking government official whose wife had died. His efforts of trying to obtain approval from the government bore no fruit. It was more difficult for him than the laterite block factory owner due to his high rank in the government. He kept trying to get permission and sending me gifts while at it. He would send me perfumes, flowers, and chocolates frequently. After a year I said no to him and his gifts too. This infuriated my brother, he stopped me from leaving the house completely, and life became a living hell. I could see his desperate attempts to get me married off.

Then came the proposal from a fisherman, extremely rich, owned a few trawlers, and buildings all around the place. He had made his money fishing offshore and then settled down to play the role of a religious scholar. He was sixty years old, had no kids, and all he had was money and the means to get approval to marry anyone he wanted to.

I recall a friend of mine telling me that the fisherman's hell would anytime be way better than my brother's heaven! This made a lot of sense to me. All I was thinking was of getting away from the clutches of my brother. My spouse's wealth and his social standing in society would help me get the freedom I so desperately sought. I knew that there would be many a challenge to face, but I was quite assured that none of it would be as devious as my brother could pose.

I said yes to the marriage!

# 2010

# 2010

# Four

They got me married on the 23rd of March!

Thinking of it now, I do not recollect the reason for having chosen Tuesday of all the days of the week for such an auspicious occasion. I see no reason other than the fact that all legal activities related to the marriage had been concluded in the court well in advance, and all that remained was to host a party for friends and relatives.

The very next day after having signed the wedding contract, I was invited along with my mother to visit the house I was to stay in. The house was quite big and spacious, when asked about how I found the house, I said that it was quite simple.

All my sisters returned to stay with us, my friends started visiting and our house became a beehive of activity. Preparations for the reception included events like henna, singing and dancing. Gifts poured in from friends and relatives. My mind, however, was fixated on nothing else than seeing the entire event as a gateway to freedom.

I wanted to move out of the clutches of my brother. The prospect of having an influential husband looked promising. I started dreaming!

Unlike any other bride, my dreams were not of affection or love, nor was it of a luxurious life but of being able to move around at my will. To be able to visit my friends when my heart desired, to continue my education, and to do my heart's bidding!

In between all the celebrations I saw my eldest sister in distress, I saw her in anguish and attributed it to my other sister having a difficult time with her family life. I was aware of her discord with her in-laws.

The marriage reception was well-attended, I remember seeing my best friend Amna dance.

I set out to live with my husband. I made the first journey to his house in his decorated car, sitting beside him as we drove home. I was in for a shock when I entered the house, I could understand my comment of the house being simple was received inappropriately and the house was refurbished with sophisticated furniture. The house had two drawing rooms, one for men and the other for women, a bedroom, and a TV room, apart from a very spacious kitchen. I could see that the carpets were ripped off and new ones laid, the walls were painted afresh, and all the furniture changed. The rooftop had a tent where he used to spend a good part of the day along with his friends. He had a big circle of friends all of whom were religious scholars. He was a very well-known and respected person and would appear frequently on television channels.

I was clueless about what remained in store for me. I knew that I had nothing more to offer than what looked back at me in the mirror, and I was grown enough to understand what men desire.

I got through the first night by requesting to be allowed to sleep in the TV room. I was relieved when he obliged and assured me that I could take my time. He slept early, woke up for the daybreak prayers and went straight to the tent on the roof along with his friends. If not in the tent on the terrace, he attended meetings with other scholars in other parts of the town, this kept him busy throughout the day and I spent time watching TV or surfing the net on my laptop.

I cooked even though the food was delivered from restaurants, he didn't want me to do the chores at home and asked me to rest and make myself comfortable.

I navigated through each day cautiously, and at night I invented excuses to sleep in the TV room alone and managed to do so for a week. It was a week of uncertainty, unsure of what the future held. Somehow, uncertainty and confusion seemed to accompany me everywhere! I could see frustration creeping in onto him, he tried to suppress his anger, but it started showing. He restrained himself and his efforts in doing so were becoming obvious.

Durrat Al-Arus was one happening place those days, a fishing village forty kilometres to the north of Jeddah, which was converted into a tourist resort. The place was known for being out of the supervision of the religious police. I still do not know what made my husband take me there, it would have been the thought that the place could loosen me up with the possibility of being delivered into his arms. The moment we reached there my eyes fell on power boats moored at the bay, I expressed my desire to sail one, and my knight at arms jumped out of the car and reappeared with the keys of a midsized boat.

I had not handled any motorised machine till then, he explained to me the controls and I sped into the darkness, into the deep sea, driving out every ounce of power from the twin engines of the boat.

With the wind in my face, speeding away from the lights of the shore, a spray of saltwater rising ahead of the boat, I tasted freedom! I loved the adrenaline rush. I clamped my jaws more from fear than from the cold spray on my face, but I loved it. I loved the speed, the fear and the darkness that engulfed me. Somewhere in between the amalgam of darkness, speed, fear and the wind, there was a sliver of death which made the experience so relaxing. I was sure that my husband would be hanging on the rail for dear life and looked over my shoulder to find him at ease, not a bit disturbed by the speed at which the boat was skimming over the water, the fisherman that he was! I had noticed a sway in his gait too, one that came from spending a long time in the sea in a small craft. So was his gaze, he had his sight locked far, cobwebs in the corner of his eyes from focusing on far-off objects. He seemed to have gained his patience by fishing alone at sea.

My life spun around on the 1st of April. I was alone in the TV room praying that he goes to bed without bothering me when I received a phone call from my sister, the one elder to me. She told me to switch the TV on and watch the program being aired. By the time I switched the TV on and flipped through the channels, the program had almost ended, and the scholar was answering the last query.

"They need help, we are bound to help them, each one of us. Society needs to ensure that they are accommodated, help must be extended to ensure that they live a normal life, it is none of their fault that they were born intersex, and medical interventions are considered permissible. They are regarded as treatment and not the altering of Allah's creation or imitation of the opposite sex." I heard the scholar saying before the program got over.

This was my moment of reckoning! The moment I realised that the way I felt was not a sin, that it was not the evil in me that made me feel as I did.

I launched myself into seeking the truth.

I had just discovered the term intersex, I started scouring the internet for whatever information I possibly could collect. I remained glued to my laptop and this started making my husband angry. He started getting frustrated and believed that my problems were a result of my remaining glued to the internet.

My mind, in turn, was closed to all other feelings than acquiring knowledge on the subject. It didn't bother me that my husband was getting restless, I was left unscathed by hunger and pain even!

The knowledge I gained in a week, saw me in a state that I had never experienced before. It was the fusion of two extremes, like ice with fire, darkness with light, noise with silence, and the calmness of the depth of the seas with the tsunami of waves.

I went through a state of profound happiness and extreme sorrow!

I was happy that the feelings I had were not ill-founded, that they had nothing to do with my faith in the Almighty being tested. I had suppressed all my longings, my craving to understand myself, to discover my physical body in fear of weakening my faith. Until then, I could never garner the courage to seek knowledge, thinking that doing so would be to question the Almighty of his creation. I feared blasphemy.

The knowledge I had gained unshackled me, led me into a state of euphoria and the thought of having lived for twenty-eight years of my life as someone who was not me, plunged me into the darkness of sorrow. I would have given anything then to stop my mind from racing, for even a few minutes. My mind sped, there was a constant thumping in my head, I even attempted to stop my breathing, to calm myself down.

On the 8th of April, a week after having watched the program on TV and two weeks after my marriage, I called my eldest sister to tell her what I had gone through in the two weeks. I heard her sobbing uncontrollably over the phone, she admitted instantly that she knew all that was happening was wrong. She went hysterical and told me that the doctor had asked me to be brought in a boy's attire for the surgery I had undergone in 1998 and that I could leave the hospital as a male, as her son Jamil had done! Our brother objected and asked the doctor to ensure that I continue to remain a female and to conduct the medical procedure accordingly.

No words will ever be able to explain the grief I went through, anger washed over me, I had not heard of bruxism till then, I realised that I was grinding my teeth when my mouth tasted odd! A sense of despair, hopelessness and total loss descended on me. I desperately wanted to believe that my brother was not aware of my condition and had hence done what he did.

10th of April, a Saturday, saw me waiting to meet the doctor who had operated on me in 1998. My sister picked me up from home on the pretext of visiting our mother and we headed straight to the hospital. The doctor had become a professor by then and was quite renowned, he had a bunch of medical students around him when he saw me. I told him that I was married, whatever the procedure he had done on me in 1998 and the medication that followed had done nothing to help me.

He retrieved my medical file, checked it, and informed me that the procedure was conducted on the basis of my personal decision and consent. Nothing could have made me madder, it felt like being consumed by a ball of fire, I went raving mad. How could I explain to anyone that I was clueless of the procedures I had gone through, that I was made to believe that I had been operated on for cancer. My emotions went haywire and for the first time ever I realised that I was screaming at a man, at the top of my voice I asked the doctor, in front of his students, if he was a butcher!

My sister and I were literally asked out of the doctor's consultation room with a promise to be met the following Saturday.

I returned home, sorrow, anger and helplessness added to the confusion that was ruling my life. I was sure of one thing though, I couldn't be anyone's wife and I told my husband exactly that.

I expected him to be shocked, but it was I who was shocked when I saw his reaction.

He started screaming. "Now, what do I tell my friends?" were the first words he uttered. I knew that quite some heroics would have been narrated in the tent on the terrace, in the days following the marriage and the concern that bothered him most was the thought of being ridiculed by his friends. Then started the bout of emotional blackmail. I was allowed as much time as was required to get comfortable, he placed no blame on me and was generous enough to suggest that it could be his misfortune and he was willing to wait it out.

Nothing anyone said made any difference to me, I just didn't care. I was in a desperate search to discover myself!

************

My brother was infuriated when he came to know of the week's developments. He was desperate for me to remain at my husband's place, and it was showing. It was becoming quite evident that he was seeing me as a threat to whatever peace was prevailing in the family.

The hope I carried, that all of what he had done was due to lack of knowledge of my condition started to fade, giving way to desperation being piled up with my worries, anger, and helplessness. I started feeling irked about my brother too. Something didn't seem right. On asking why he had given consent for the sex correction procedure that was conducted on me in 1998, he said that the chromosome test conducted then had revealed 98% XY chromosomes with 1% chromosome damaged, hence, it was quite logical that treatment be done to ensure that I develop feminine traits and physique. I appeared for a chromosome test again and was shocked by the results. The results showed 100% XY chromosomes, the doctor was shocked beyond belief too. He stated that one of the results was wrong as there existed no possibility of change occurring in chromosomes, no matter when the test was conducted. I had no doubt about which test was false, for the second one was done by me in person.

My brother then said that I suffered from testosterone allergy. Getting a testosterone allergy test done was not an easy affair then, but I managed to get it done and had to wait for a fortnight for the results as the samples had to be sent to Germany. I waited in horror for the results, each hour seemed like a day, I could hardly sleep at night and was pleasantly surprised when the tests came out negative. He then said that I had ovaries, it took just one ultrasound scan to prove otherwise.

It dawned on me that it would be idiotic to turn to my brother for help.

On the 1st of May, I packed my bags and returned to stay with my mother. My brother wanted me to return to my husband's house. He told him that I had come home to look after my mother and would return to his place soon. I didn't much bother about what was going on between them and had my heart set on meeting the doctor.

I started making rounds of the hospital, settling myself down comfortably in the waiting room where the doctor would spot me on his way in and out, patiently waiting for the doctor to call me. I had perfected the art of waiting, I could exhibit utmost calmness and the willingness to wait through the day, making whoever I was waiting for, uneasy. The doctor called me in once, just to tell me to return after a week.

One day when I was turned back asking to return later, I decided to write the doctor an email. It stated—

*May the peace and mercy of God Almighty be on you.*

*Dear doctor,*

*Before I delve into the matter, allow me to introduce myself to you. I had come to the hospital a while ago because of the problems I have been suffering from, since the year 1998, after the sex correction surgery you conducted on me.*

*Doctor, this month so far has weighed very heavy on me, it has been one of the most difficult months in my life. I feel that a fellow human being has been betrayed because of my condition.*

*I am a person who believes in God, my day starts with praising him, I praise him throughout the day and that is the last thing I do before I retire for the night. I do not lament on his decree, nor do I object to what God has willed for me. I am thankful to him for everything.*

*I turn to you now as the fog has started to clear, what has been hidden throughout the past years is becoming clearer. I just can't explain what this uncertainty has been doing to me, how it has been eating me out from the inside. It has made me hollow while I desperately try to hang on, living a day at a time, holding on by the sheer strength of my faith and prayers.*

*For a long time, I have experienced masculine tendencies, but I have remained unable to speak about it as I have been living my whole life thinking that the problem existed in my mind. I have developed skills to push such thoughts away from my mind and suppress them even before they germinate. I have been living a life of torture. I swear by God Almighty, the efforts to control my feelings when I am among females, tire me out. Try as I may, this faithful servant of God gets swayed by lust, and I find myself amid a whirlpool.*

*Doctor, only God understands my medical condition completely, after him, it is you, and men are subject to error, aren't they?*

*Let me try explaining to you that due to the environment I have been raised in, my childhood and adolescence differed from that of a normal youth. My mother's mental illness refrained us from speaking out about our problems for fear of what would happen to our mother. It wasn't only me, all of us at home learned to bear our pain in silence. We buried our secrets within, we were taught to think of others and were forced to believe that thinking of ourselves is a sin.*

*I was seventeen when you conducted the sex correction surgery on me, I swear by God Almighty that I was not informed of what the surgery was for nor was I aware of the consequences. I sat for a while looking at the scar and assumed that what would have been removed would be cancer about which I had heard my folks talk. I had no reason to suspect. Why would I?*

*I do not repent the years I have lost; I consider that to be God's decree. Now that I have started to acquire knowledge of my condition and have understood the reason for my suffering all these years, I realize that the feelings I had were not abnormal or sinful.*

*I am content with what has been and place no blame on anyone for my state, but I want common sense to take its course, remove my bosom and wean me off the hormones that made them grow in the first place, I can feel them destroying my bones and weakening me greatly. Let me live my life in peace, even if I remain unable to get married.*

*Dear doctor, I request you to consider doing a fellow human being a favour, please take a second look at my condition and get me out of the living hell that I currently am in.*

*I will complete all the required documentation however difficult it might be. I am sure that my Lord will not disappoint me, because I seek his guidance before I take any step and beg him to guide me on the right path.*

*May God Almighty reward you in abundance.*

The days that followed were spent in anxiety; my brother tried to convince me that what was done was in the best of interest for me. When he was not able to convince me with logic, he tried to do so by quoting religion. I begged him to support me by helping me do what I wanted done and not by trying to tell me what I need to do. He told me that the first thing that needs to be done to start getting things in order is for me to return to my husband's house.

I listened to him! I went back to his house, made him sit with me and told him the entire story. He continued to say that we could both live together in the house and went to the extent of trying to convince me that he would not live beyond two to three months. I could wait for him to die and then inherit all his wealth and do whatever I wished to do.

As strange as it all sounded, waiting for someone's death to commence my life was beyond what I could comprehend. I collected my personal documents, my jewellery, my computer, and left the house the next morning. I returned to my mother's house.

My husband called up my brother and they both agreed that I was being reckless. I needed to keep silent and continue to live at my husband's place to safeguard the social standing of both families, they said. My brother was very angry when I told him that there was no way for me to continue as someone's wife. I was clear that I wouldn't let anyone take decisions on my behalf and I would not fall prey to any emotional blackmail stating my mother's illness.

It was made clear to me by my brother that he would not help me in any manner until I returned to my husband. The old man didn't want to divorce me, and it suited my brother well. As long as I remained married to him, I would not be able to do anything without his consent. My husband had his reputation to guard, my brother found it difficult to understand how someone could be as selfish as me, and there was the family's reputation at stake. How could I be so inconsiderate of my sister's children, and his children too, who will have to get married.

My attempts to gain freedom by marrying seemed to have failed. I wouldn't be able to step out of the house if my husband willed so!

The urge to give up was compelling. To just let go of everything and continue to live as I was doing, not to think about anything and let the surroundings take control. To live as a woman, not to question my feelings and train myself not to think. To reconcile to my lot.

I knew that I had hit the bottom of the pit, I knew that this was the darkest it could get, I could either give up and let the darkness consume me or chose to fight back. One thought that came to me at the lowest point in my life, at the darkest hour, was to call my friend Amna. I saw a ray of hope after having talked to her, she assured me that I had every reason to fight back, to decide for myself, and most importantly, to live.

Amna brought hope, and shone a ray of light into the darkness that engulfed me, she became the reason for me to hang on with whatever strength I had remaining in me.

On one of the first few days after marriage, my husband had shown me the pen with a camera which he always carried in his pocket to record clips and produce as evidence when and if required. I listened to his heroics and realised how very mean he could be. I have learnt in life that the way a person does something is the way he does everything. I remember making a mental note and scanning all the rooms for hidden cameras or bugs.

One morning, I called him on the phone requesting for divorce, explaining to him that I was more a male than a female. He told me that he didn't intend to divorce me as he was comfortable living with me. I reiterated that I am a male to which he responded that he liked boys and would be happy to continue living with me.

I called him again the next morning and played back the previous day's recording. There was silence on the other side of the line, not a word was spoken, and I cut the line. He called me after a while threatening me, wanting to know how dare I record the call. I remained calm and in an ice-cold voice asked him to imagine the outcome when the voice clip will be uploaded on the websites where he was making his scholarly speeches.

I would never do such a thing in my life, I couldn't even imagine blackmailing someone, but I was cornered, I would either have to submit myself or fight my way out. I decided to do the latter.

I got my divorce the very next day & went to perform Haj pilgrimage with my mother and sisters.

I returned from the pilgrimage to start a new life. A life for which I knew I would have to fight. I would have to cut my past away and build a brand new one right from the very beginning.

Like the nomads who lived on the steppes of Almaty, I decided to forget my past, unburden myself of all that belonged there and live in the present.

***********

I was back at the doctor's place, patiently waiting for my consultation. As was usual, I was seen after the last patient had left and his students were dispersed. I told the doctor that my marriage was over, I wanted to do the right thing now, the right thing for myself, I wanted to do what I knew was right and not what anyone else decided for me with their convenience in mind. The doctor gave me a patient listen and asked me to return after two years with a firm decision. "You are back after twelve years of having undergone a sex correction surgery, we cannot be making a mistake again, think about it for the next two years and then return with your decision." He promised to help me out when and if I returned.

I had absolutely no doubt that I would return, nor about what I wanted done, but decided to agree to wait for two years just to assure the doctor that I was not taking any reckless decision. The wait was anything but easy, I would walk down the street just to keep myself busy and even time was merciless to me, it seemed to stand still. Sitting idle made the condition worse. I was born with the trait of being fidgety, remaining inactive makes me overthink. It applies to the way I sleep too; I can sleep peacefully with the music playing, I do not wake up to noise but would spring out of bed if someone would try to pussyfoot into the room.

My brother continued to oppose my decision. He, not only refused to help but disowned me saying that he was not my brother anymore, nor was I, his sister.

Grim as it might have sounded, I disagreed, to him not being my brother but agreed that I was not his sister. "I am your brother!" was all I could tell him.

I had given up all hopes of expecting help from him and told him that I would discontinue my hormone therapy medications.

The Premarin tablets that were prescribed to me were a part of feminizing hormone therapy which left my skin hairless and smooth, my bones soft and made my bosom protrude, while it gave me regular stomach upsets, bloating, tenderness in my breasts, severe mood swings, depression, and lack of sleep. I would remain unable to attribute it left on my emotions. It hurt very bad, it hurt where one couldn't inspect the wound.

I never expected life to be easy, nor did I desire my days to be filled with sunshine always, but this hormone could make everything seem gloomy and dull.

My brother resorted to writing emails to me so that he could address all my sisters also in the communication.

Following is an email written by him on the 25th day of May 2010, trying to convince me to continue the medication.

Regarding the Premarin tablets that you are taking, if you read the prescription, you will find that it is a replacement hormone that provides estrogen only. There are other types of hormone replacement therapy medications that differ from the composition of Premarin.

One important fact that you need to understand is that the human body, be it male or female requires estrogen, which in your case is provided by Premarin that you consume. As you are a female, estrogen required by your body is supposed to be naturally produced by the uterus and ovaries. The absence of both these organs causes a complete lack of estrogen, hence it is imperative that you continue the medication.

As regarding its effect on bones, estrogen is a stimulant that helps maintain bone density and strengthens it. Unlike what you think, it does not cause pain or calcium deficiency.

You will be able to find numerous articles that explain the importance of estrogen, and how it assists the bones in a woman's body, especially during the time she matures and during menopause. As I have stated earlier, estrogen is not produced by your body and must be substituted through regular intake of Premarin. You need to understand the symptoms that women who enter menopause or who, for medical reasons, have their uterus removed go through, as estrogen is no longer produced in their body. I suggest that you try to understand postmenopausal symptoms before you decide on discontinuing your medication.

In summation, what I wish to tell you is that the Premarin you are taking is pure estrogen without the presence of any other *hormones. You would have investigated ones with other hormones in it and arrived at a wrong conclusion.*

The email made me more frustrated and desperate, to say the least.

I was trying to explain that the hormones I was taking were hurting me, that I was not a woman, and my brother was trying to convince me otherwise. It seemed like pleading a brick wall for help, you may scream at the top of your voice, you may tear your throat apart screaming, but your voice won't carry. It reminded me of a dream that used to reoccur when I was a kid. A dream where I was trying to escape from a monster advancing on me. I used to go breathless trying to run but the monster kept advancing, gaining on me. I remember sitting up in bed sweating!

Here I was trying to forget the past and live the day, but my brother made it impossible.

When he saw that his medical jargon failed to move me, he tried convincing me that what I was doing was wrong from a religious point of view, that I might be going against God's will and committing a crime on myself.

An excerpt from one of his emails read as follows—

*Way before any decision was taken, do you know what the doctor did? He administered male hormones to you, it is only after your body rejected the male hormones that we decide that your sex needs to remain female. It was quite evident that your cells do not accept male hormones despite the presence of XY chromosomes in your body. The only way remaining was to ensure that you develop female attributes and hence the surgery was conducted.*

*Now when you tell me that you are a male, not a female and the sex correction surgery that had happened should have been to change you into a male, I request you to give thought to what I have said. If your cells refuse to accept male hormones and you have thoughts of becoming a male, you might be going against God's will.*

*Do ask forgiveness from your Lord and seek refuge in Him.*

*Do not commit a crime on yourself and on everyone around you.*

As I have stated earlier, none of these could sway me. I got a testosterone allergy test done, even though it required sending the samples to Germany and the test results were negative.

I decided to make it clear to my brother that I had lost faith in him and did so by writing an email with all my sisters copied, just like he was doing.

*Ahmed, do you know what your problem is? You seem to arrive at conclusions with very shallow knowledge of the subject.*

*You first told me that I am suffering from mixed gonadal dysgenesis, you went to explain further that I had ovaries, and at a later stage told me that it is due to lack of ovaries that I must remain on estrogen supplement medication, and you assured me that you had spent several hours with the doctors trying to understand my condition.*

*Ahmed, I just can't tell you how very grateful I felt for your concern, and how I thanked God for having blessed me with a brother like you. I saw you as a ray of hope in my otherwise dark and depressing life.*

*As has been the case with happiness that has ever come my way, this too was short-lived.*

*I cannot really explain what I went through when the doctor I met read out my medical test report saying that I have absolutely no trace of mixed gonadal dysgenesis. I was caught between being happy for not having the disease, and sad, thinking about how you could commit such a mistake. I was not sure if it was ignorance, then.*

*Later, when you told me that I am suffering from testicular feminization syndrome, I felt at a total loss! How could these doctors you see, read reports so carelessly? Don't we care for stray cats more? Wouldn't they realize that the judgement they are making would affect a human being's life? A human being who is fighting a war not to win over others, nor seek fame or fortune but to live whatever is remaining of my life without being pumped with hormones and medications.*

*I wish I could make you understand how it makes me feel when I take Premarin tablets, and how it hurts me physically and mentally. What it does to my whole body and the depression it plunges my mind into. I pray very hard during those moments to God Almighty to give me the strength to overcome the loathing and to give me the courage and the will to live.*

*Yet another concern you have raised is about altering God's creation.*

*I pray we become a little empirical here. My Lord has created me deformed and I accept his will. I suffer patiently in silence, but the greatest suffering is when people who have shared the same womb fail to acknowledge my suffering and accept that I too have a right to live.*

*Is it not a little absurd that you have concluded by yourself that I am a female and that I should be treated like how a normal female is done? Does the Shariah law not encourage even surgery to be conducted if so advised by medical experts to ascertain the true sex, so that the person can be designated a certain gender in order for him or her to be able to have a good life and able to perform his or her duties as a Muslim?*

*I have very little to say other than that I pray to God Almighty to safeguard you and your children from what ails me. May he not make you suffer for a day, what I have been suffering all through my life.*

*All I ask for, is to be considered a human being, do not subject me to medical experiments which would prove wrong after fifty years by which time I would have spent my life in pain and mental agony.*

*When I have been telling you that I have XY chromosomes and that I felt like a boy all through my adolescent years, all I expect you to do is to stand by me. I do not expect you to lecture me otherwise. Who else would know what goes in my mind and body better than I do? Doesn't the religion-state clearly that if the person experiences feelings like a male after maturity, then he will be counted as a male?*

*But alas, you are stubborn and arrogant! You think that you know what is best for me and in seeking the best for me, you are influenced by the thought of how society will react, the future of your children and the alliances of your daughters when they come of age.*

*I have resolved that I will stop my current medication, and none other than God Almighty and myself would know my body better. I have decided to decide for myself. I will wait for the medical reports before I proceed.*

*My Lord is with me, and I am assured that he will not disappoint me.*

*May He help me to find the truth and follow in its path, may He keep me away from falsehood and guard me against all evil.*

*May God Almighty forgive me and you, for any mistakes that would have happened on our part.*

*I rest, thanking God for all that has been bestowed on me till now!*

Forgetting the past and living in the future was not enough, I decided that I have had enough of living in a make-believe world, and I resolved to fight my battle all alone. Not that I was unaware of the uphill climb or the walls that I would face in the process. I knew that tackling the medical part was just one aspect and I would have to handle the religious aspect, in addition to obtaining permission from my guardian as is required by the law of the land.

I would not let any thought weaken my resolve and kept clearing every obstacle that thwarted my progress.

It was during one of the several meetings I had with the doctor that I met Sumer.  I was alone in the doctor's room waiting for him to return when the door opened, and a girl peeped in. Never until then, nor ever after have I seen the iris diaphragm of a person shiver! She was extremely nervous. I stood up by instinct and was instantly taken aback when she asked me, "Are you intersex too?" She took my phone number and left. I could see that she had come with her father, unlike me!

I should admit that I was not sure at the time. I suspected the chance meeting with Sumer to be a ploy by my brother to try to influence my decisions, and hence I was reluctant to share information, however friendly she was trying to be over the phone.

Later I realized that I was becoming suspicious by nature and it would never help my attempts of trying to discard the past.

I became careful not to dehumanize those who disagreed with me. In my self-righteousness, I didn't wish to become the very person that I was feeling sick of, and not even know it.

I wrote to my sisters, summing up the progress I had till then.

*My dear sisters,*

*I would like to update you on the progress that I have had to date.*

*I got a chromosomal analysis done and the results came out 100% XY, this as you all know, is contrary to the results that were furnished to the doctor when he conducted my sex correction surgery in 1998.*

*When I took the latest results to the doctor, he was dumbfounded and all he had to say is that one of the results is wrong! We all know that the chromosomes in a person can't change over a period of time, and I am left with no doubt as to which of the results is incorrect.*

*I had discussed with him how to proceed with the treatment and what would be required to do so, he was worried about the legal rulings and had requested me to wait till he seeks legal advice. Thankfully, he got back to me saying that there would be no legal problems, but a committee would be formed to enquire into the case, the first medical procedure that was conducted and the hormone treatment that followed.*

*The doctor and I have agreed to postpone the treatment till I solve the problem of a guardian authorising the procedure. I am convinced that I will not receive any help from our brother, nor he would grant consent for the surgery.*

*As a result of all the meetings I had with the doctor, I decided to get an official fatwa that would help with what I wanted to do. I wrote in detail to General Mufti and other accredited sheikhs and received the fatwa permitting me to undergo the surgery and treatment that would follow.*

*Now, the challenge of getting consent from a guardian looms like a mountain before me. After having spoken to a few lawyers and a judge, I have submitted a request to the royal court, along with the fatwa, to permit me to represent myself, based on the fatwa issued and I have challenged the medical procedure that was conducted on me in 1998 without my knowledge.*

*I see the progress as rays of hope and pray to God Almighty to bless my efforts!*

My emotions started running haywire again, my attempts to smile resulted in frowns and my facial muscles ached! The medications or discontinuation of some would have been the cause for me feeling the way I did. I have always believed that there is a bard in everyone, the one in me decided to write. The first of my scribbles read—

*What should I write?*

*How do I say that I want to cry?*

*How do I say that I need a hand to help me, one to comfort me?*

*My life floats like a kite with its thread severed, sans control.*

*I yearn to laugh, to dance, to return to the simplicity of my life.*

*I fear that it is all over,*

*I wonder, is laughter an emotion from the past?*

*Am I lost somewhere in my journey; am I straying from my path?*

*How long have I been walking, and why is it that I do not have my destination in sight yet?*

*Oh, Lord, I am tired!*

*I am tired of treading alone.*

*How I wish that I had a shoulder to lean on.*

*Someone to hold me and for me to hold.*

*How I wish I could hug someone to sleep,*

*With nothing else than the love of this world in my heart!*

Such were my feelings those days. A sense of despair, lethargy, nightmares, emotional difficulties, depresssion, and a lack of spontaneous interest in the surroundings. I was struggling within myself to keep the fight on and praying hard that I remain sane while at it. Writing started to soothe me, words formed in my head, not that they rhymed nor was there any reason, but I wrote to calm my troubled self, down.

*They think,*

*They think I forgot,*

*They think I am done,*

*They think I am lost.*

*They think I don't care anymore,*

*They think I have reconciled to my lot!*

*They think that I don't even think of what they have done to me.*

*They think, but they do not know.*

*How would they know?*

*They have not lived a day what I have lived a lifetime.*

*Devoid of the most valuable of God's bounties.*

*As simple and worthless as it might seem to them, or any human being.*

*Identity and freedom!*

*Not worth a speck of salt if you have them.*

*Not what a mountain of gold can buy if you don't.*

*I have neither money nor gold,*

*But I have set forth seeking both.*

*I have the fight in me, I have the struggle.*

*I have God by me in my travel.*

*In him, I believe and on him, I rely to attain my goal.*

*To live my life the way I wish.*

*To live my life the way I dream.*

*Not as they wish, not as they dream.*

*Not as they think I should.*

*They think I am exaggerating,*

*They think I am ungrateful.*

*They think, but they don't realize,*

*But then, how would they?*

*How would they realize, they have not lived a day what I have lived a lifetime.*

*I beg my lord not to afflict them with what I have been afflicted with.*

*All I wish is—*

*They don't think,*

*They don't judge me,*

*They don't decide for me.*

*Just let me decide.*

*You may think as much as you may,*

*But you won't know me.*

*Don't think, just support me!*

I was reaching out for help, I wanted someone to understand me, to help me without judging me, I could feel gloom descending on me, robbing me of whatever happiness I had in my life.

*For years we did not part,*

*You lived by my heart,*

*Did we not comfort each other?*

*Sometimes you would disappear, just to appear again!*

*After having made my heart beat faster.*

*You would leave, but return in a day, if not in hours!*

*But recently you have disappeared.*

*I looked through the hour, through the day, through the summer and all through winter.*

*I looked for you by day, I looked for you by night.*

*You seem to have left, not to return!*

*Your absence hurts, you have been away for long.*

*Don't you see me searching for you as a shepherd who goes out in search of his missing lamb?*

*Only that he leaves his ninety-nine unattended,*

*But I have none other than you!*

*There was a time when you and I were like the body and soul,*

*We never would separate from each other.*

*The absence of one necessitated the death of the other!*

*Nature seems to have been envious of our harmony,*

*For I see no other reason for you having left with my smile.*

*Leaving my body barren of its soul!*

*I live, I eat, I drink, I breathe,*

*But I feel nothing!*

*I have become a madman, looking for you in the streets,*

*I look for you in the market, even in the corners of the house!*

*But you seem to have disappeared without a trace,*

*Knowing well enough that I will come in search of you.*

*This is a call for all who read my lines,*

*To join me in looking for my missing half.*

*For four eyes are better than two, and a dozen hearts better than one.*

*If at all you find him before I do, tell him to hasten back,*

*His absence has rendered me insane!*

*Oh Happiness, come back to me.*

*For with you, I am nothing!*

*I eat, I drink, I breathe... but I feel nothing!*

Faith was what kept me going, no matter how difficult or stressful the times turned out to be. With every obstacle I encountered, my faith in God Almighty increased and I came out stronger and more determined. It was only due to faith that suicidal thoughts never germinated in my mind, death seemed like a blessing at some point in time though. I recall witnessing a road accident, I saw rib bones sticking out of white starched shirt and realizing later that I was unmoved by the sight of death. I penned down the incident.

*How can fear and indolence live in harmony?*

*I never thought this possible.*

*Until I realized that both dwell in me, in peace!*

*Each, not only in acceptance but in appreciation of the other!*

*A wave of panic hits me, doused by a state of gloom.*

*I happened to witness a terrible traffic accident today,*

*I knew someone had lost his life,*

*I was not sad nor was I scared.*

*I felt nothing.*

*The only thing I was worried about was that I was not affected!*

*Had death become dear to me?*

*Did I see comfort in the leveller?*

*Was death the highest form of Lord's mercy?*

*If not to those left behind but from whom the soul departed,*

*An end to misery in this mortal world.*

*To live in comfort ever after with the Lord,*

*The most merciful, the most beneficent!*

*But why am I feeling the way I do?*

*Has indolence overtaken fear?*

*Am I falling in love with darkness? Slipping into depression?*

*Am I losing one more emotion?*

*Even fear seems too dear when it comes to losing!*

*Why am I not afraid of anyone, anymore?*

*Nor of what people think of me.*

*All that scares me is myself,*

*My thoughts, my intentions, and the path that I am treading on.*

*Am I on the right track, what awaits me at the end of the road?*

*I won't know till I arrive but tread I will.*

*You meet a few on your journey,*

*You leave some who don't matter,*

*Live they may, but not to you, to you they are as good as dead!*

*There's many a dead one among the living.*

*Many continue to live even after they have left!*

The start of the two years wait was the most stressful, it was not just waiting but winning many a battle, the fiercest being the one my heart was having with my brain.

I decided to start working again, I was ready to take a man's job, and this turned out to be the real transition of my life!

# 2011

# 2011

# Five

I was walking briskly down the road, headed nowhere, trying to delink the chain of thoughts snaking through my mind. I put one foot in front of the other and tried to concentrate on nothing else other than focusing on moving forward. I was scared of the pressure on my brain leading me to something that was beyond my control.

It was a factory that made plastic lids for water gallons. A friend of mine worked there and she called me to inform me that the place had a vacancy for an office administrator. I presented myself for the job.

The Premarin tablets, however depressing they were to consume, pushed out my bosom and made me look full-bodied. The 'abhaya' we girls wore concealed the whole body, but for the part of hands beneath the wrists and the eyes. The anticipation of what lay beyond added pace to the Egyptian manager's decision making and it took only minutes for him to offer me the position.

I was like a galley slave unshackled, working through the day to keep myself occupied. Within the first few weeks, I had the office fully organised, with all documents filed and in order. The month that followed saw me communicating with suppliers, maintaining customer records, planning sales, monitoring cash flow, and working on the welfare of the factory workers. Within three months I had gained knowledge of the machinery and could easily supervise production.

I was thoroughly enjoying my work but unfortunately the manager who had recruited me had done so in expectation of personal favours, way over efficiency at work!

It was quite evident that he saw me as a threat to his employment but the lascivious possibilities that he dreamt of forced him to take the risk of letting me continue! It did not last long though and he started making it obvious that I was not welcome if it was only work that I had to offer. I started getting my first lessons about the man's world. I could see through him and make him seek cover with my gaze! I enjoyed making him uncomfortable but ended up losing my job.

Losing the job did not bother me for an instant as I was determined to establish my own business, even though I had not a penny on me.

I had the know-how and the confidence in me to raise capital. Armed with a good presentation, I raised close to a million Saudi Rials to set up the business with 25% shares of the company as my working partnership without financial investment.

The machinery was imported from China, and the factory was set up in the industrial zone in Jeddah. Yet again, what the Premarin tablets had done to me helped in obtaining approvals and licences way faster than it would have been otherwise. In three months, the line was functional and ready to produce. These were three months of restless toil without any break. I literally slept at the premises, I learnt to drive too even though women were not allowed to drive. The industrial city was quite empty, and I drove inside the zone. Lifting the foot off the brake and accelerating away brought such jubilant a feeling, like that of unshackling the chains and escaping into freedom. At last, I started experiencing freedom, nothing I had tasted until then seemed as sweet!

I manned the factory with the help of a few labourers who were employed on daily wages. We produced the first few batches of plastic lids. Production went as planned but the product lacked quality, and the stocks we had supplied started getting returned from the market, doubling our logistic costs. I knew that changing the moulds would solve the problem, but my partners started to panic. They refused to invest any more money and suggested disposing the factory instead. The key investors being my sister's in-laws, I had to handle the affair very delicately. It didn't take me much time to realize my mistake of having chosen partners for their financial capacities over business acumen.

Attempts to churn out better quality products with faulty equipment kept me engaged. These challenges did not bother me much, I was confident that I would be able to obtain better quality with a little bit of tweaking. Letting go so easily was not an option for me. Stress and pressure at work did not affect me, both being a part of my life right from when I could recall, they served in helping me disconnect from my personal issues. I worked day and night trying to set the factory right but to no avail.

I learnt swimming against the current, handling objections and most important of all, I got insights into the man's world! My brother did not bother me much, he let me be, knowing that I would have to return to take permission from him if I wanted to get any personal affair done. The law of the land required that a female obtain permission from her guardian even to travel beyond the district borders.

I started practising and enjoying my new skills at man-watching. I had the perseverance to sit for hours and observe, many a time making the subject of my observation so uncomfortable that they would do anything to see me off, which included granting licences and permissions which was required to run my business.

The year prepared me to understand the world I wished to enter. I knew that I would lose the preference I currently enjoyed when I would enter the man's world as a man. I would have to take the longer queues and be ready to be treated like anyone else in the crowd. I will have to be ready to reach the teller at the bank after waiting for hours, just to be asked to return after the prayer break. I knew life would change, I would have to leave all my old friends behind, they would not want to associate with me, I would not have what everyone else reveres most when they grow old, and I would not have friends from my childhood. I would have to leave all of them behind and I would not be able to make friends, at least not the sort of friends one makes at the age one doesn't judge. It all seemed a little scary, but nothing would stop me from accepting any challenge, making any sacrifice, or bearing any amount of pain to regain my actual identity.

I should admit, that at times, returned the urge to let everything go, to just give up the fight and live each day as it comes. Having got married, I could even have had a life partner and lived in luxury till fate took whatever turn it had to take. In doing so, I would have continued to remain dear to my brother. But yes, one would have to wait and see what fate held in store. To think that I would live without being bothered would be to dwell in a fool's paradise. If I knew any, I knew that a time would come when I would be expected to provide what a wife provides to her husband. Regardless of I not being able to develop any feelings for a male partner, plastic surgeons would accomplish what would be required by my husband.

Even the thought of cooking for a man and seeing him eat to his heart's content failed to bring any sort of relief to me. I had learned to cook but seeing someone eat made no difference to me, unlike what I had heard many a women say. "There is nothing more pleasing than watching your man eat what you have cooked, not even making love," I've heard them say when we used to party at the weekends, but my thoughts revolved around being fed, rather than cooking for someone.

I had nothing more to lose, I couldn't even boast of a gender for myself, I ceased to be emotionally blackmailed by my brother, and I sought no help from him.

Having nothing to lose, no one to fear, and none to please, I understood that I was free to choose my destiny.

# 2013

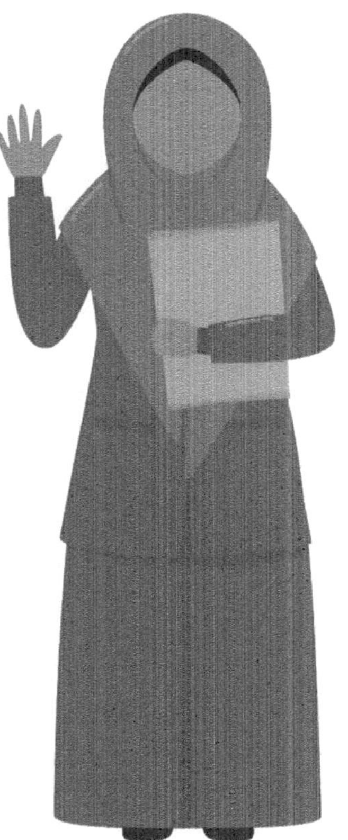

# 2013

# Six

Equipped with all the new skills and knowledge I had gathered, I visited the doctor again in the month of July. I was back to assure him that I was firm on my decision. I could see that he had no other choice than to be convinced that I was clear with my objectives and asked me to return with my guardian.

Obstinacy runs in our family, and it still does. I would do anything but not ask my brother for help. He had categorically stated that I should not expect any assistance or help from him, and I was hell-bent on not accepting any. I had foreseen this obstacle and had sought permission from the court to represent myself. The *fatwa* I had obtained helped me file such a request, but it did not go any further than that, nor had I followed up on the matter. A female seeking permission to represent herself would have been quite unheard of and the court granting such a permission would be quite impossible unless the plaintiff would have been legitimately represented by a team of lawyers. I had no means of affording a lawyer, leave alone a team of them.

I put my skills to work again and convinced the doctor that I could get my uncle instead of my brother to sign the consent. It took quite some deliberation but at the end of it all, the doctor, though with a sigh of reluctance, gave in!

My uncle was a jeweller, his handmade jewellery was well-known amongst the elite population of the country. He had a way with pearls and stones and very high level of expertise in setting them in gold. His persona matched his craftmanship. 'Flawless' is one word that would depict him and hence he was not on the best of terms with my brother.

I found it easy to explain my situation to him, he was shocked, he knew about my nephew Jamil and was lost trying to find one good reason why the same was not done with me. Not only did he accompany me to the hospital, but he also made sure that the doctor had no doubts remaining by the time we left.

"Come back after a week and meet the plastic surgeon for a preliminary check," said the doctor. I could not believe my ears, if not for my veil he would have seen me weep! Weep tears of joy! I spent the week in anticipation, often reassuring myself that all of what was happening is real, that I am not dreaming. I knew that the mind could play tricks at times, it had done so many times when I was on medication, but this was real. The doctor had finally agreed to set things right, to correct the mistake committed fifteen years back. The doctor was at the peak of his career, and he was risking tarnishing his credentials too by admitting that such a medical blunder had been committed. I did not doubt that it was my prayers that melted his heart.

I was back the next week even before the sun was out! It was one of the most beautiful daybreaks, each ray of the sun carried hope. The surgeon examined me for a good two hours, "We will call you back, and you need to come prepared to stay for a week," he declared. No specific date was given but I was asked to expect a call soon. I shivered, my lips trembled, I lost my appetite, and my heart felt light. I spent time praying and thanking God for his mercy.

I did receive a call the very next week, not from the hospital but from my friend Sumer, she had received an appointment from the hospital for her plastic surgery, the first of a series of three medical procedures one had to go through for sex correction. I volunteered to stay with her in the hospital while she went through the process, the surgery took eight hours, and it was not a pretty sight when they rolled her out of the theatre. Tubes crisscrossed her body and bags hung all around the bed. Recovery was quite quick, and she was able to walk the very next day.

I stayed with Sumer for all the seven days and saw her leave the hospital as Sameer, dressed as a man! Sumer's parents had come to take Sameer back and emotions ran quite high. I was confused too, no one would expect me to be friends with Sameer, not in our culture, at least not until I would become a man! Suddenly, our friendship had to end, I tried to reason what name I would give to such a relationship, a friendship when someone transitions through gender! The last of the thoughts I shared with him before he left the hospital was not to look for anything in the past.

I desperately wanted a break; I told my mother and travelled to Riyadh to live with my sister. I could feel my heart racing all the while, my nerves jumping. I sought solace in scribbling as I usually did—

*Wide, though narrow.*

*As beautiful as she is ugly,*

*Generous in all her greed!*

*The suffocation in her embrace...*

*This is our world, so where do we escape?*

*Why do we complain about it?*

*We pray, and we cry when we pray.*

*When it comes to us, we reject it.*

*When stubborn, we seek it!*

*She deprives us, and we curse her might.*

*We explored and left her exposed.*

*We chose to complain about her oppression,*

*But love is what we expect in return!*

*We hate her, we love her, we hate her again,*

*She remains beloved no matter how much we hate,*

*And marches away taking our lives!*

*We cling to her until our last breath, and until the last day of our wretched lives.*

*Cursing yesterday, cursing every hour of the day!*

*We complain about how unjust she has been to us when we are the ones who have wronged her!*

*How do we seek forgiveness for having sinned against you?*

*We the mortals promise to be better than we are,*

*We live as we want to live,*

*We, who are created from soil and to your soil we shall return.*

*We will stop complaining about your injustice and remain grateful for what you have to offer.*

*We, who are your guests,*

*We, who have come to go!*

*And you remain stable to receive many a guest like us.*

*Pray, you let us thank you for all that we have taken from you,*

*And let us leave contented that we paid our dues!*

I wrote, more to keep my hand busy than to seek words to pen down, words seemed to parade down in unending ranks, like ants marching down a windowsill from within a crack in the wood into the patch of sunlight.

I woke up one morning to the ring of my phone, the call was from the hospital asking me to report for surgery the very next day.

The fact that I was in Riyadh suited me well, I flew back to Jeddah the same evening, got myself admitted to the hospital, called up my mother and told her that I would stay in Riyadh longer. No one other than my sisters and my friend Amna was aware of the progress.

I can recollect being carted into the operation theatre exactly at the stroke of '9'. Amna followed me up to the door of the theatre. She had left home for work and came to the hospital instead. Amna somehow happened to be my ray of light in pitch dark, she would appear from nowhere before I hit the bottom of the pit. A star that shone bright when the night was the darkest!

As the anaesthesia started taking control of me, I started drifting to a land unknown, miles of meadows, a gurgling stream, tiny yellow flowers, millions of them, tossing and dancing in the breeze! I could feel the embalming sun on my face, it left honey-coloured patches on the brook. The breeze was scented with the aroma of wild blossoms, clove, and milk.

I could hear Amna sing! I looked for her between the towering grass, in the shade of the giant tree, but she was nowhere in sight. I could hear her though and her scent came floating in.

I surfaced and the first thing I saw, even before noticing that I had lost my bosom and rubber tubes protruding out of the rib cage, was Amna looking at me, concern written all over her face. I was on the other side of an eight-hour-long surgery, unsure, but relieved to step back into reality. I could see my sister weeping when I enquired about our mother. In my semi-conscious state of mind, I felt guilty for not having offered Namaz. I was particular about praying on time right from when I was a kid and would not let any worldly affairs refrain me from doing so. I knew and continue to believe that it is my faith in religion that has helped me not to fall apart. I would have been torn to shreds if not for my faith in God Almighty.

My eldest sister came to stay over for the night relieving Amna who returned to the hospital to stay by me during the day. For the first time in my life, I received a gift meant for the male gender. Amna gifted me a 'Polo Red' perfume. I remained in bed for six days. When my mother called on the phone, we managed to route the calls through my sister in Riyadh, who told her that I am around and would then call up Amna who would wake me up to return the call. I had decided not to inform my mother and had warned all my sisters against doing so, for fear of her health deteriorating. We didn't disclose it to our brother as it would have done more harm than help.

On the sixth day, I was informed of a minor medical procedure that I had to undergo before I could leave for home. They rolled me back into the theatre to pull out the rubber tubes that protruded from both sides of my chest, I am yet not sure where the ends were lodged within me. I remember the doctor and a nurse holding the tube to the left of me and asking me to take a deep breath. I was mid-way when I felt a piercing pain knife through my whole body! It originated somewhere in my heart and travelled to every part of my body, only to return where it had set forth from. I have never experienced such pain. Not before, nor after. I hovered over the limits of my pain threshold and was not lucky enough to lose consciousness. On recovering my senses, I could hear the doctor say that I had held on well while he was busy closing the puncture with sutures. It felt as if they had plucked out my toenails. It was when they moved to my right that I realised that the horror was not over. The one to the right was yet to be removed. If not for the sense of victory that came with the pain, I would not have survived. But there prevailed a sense of achievement, of having beaten the odds and a smile germinated on my face catching the doctor off guard. He slapped my face to ensure that I had not lost consciousness and was shocked when I told him to pull the other tube out!

We left the hospital for my sister's house. Unlike my friend Sumer, I wore the cloak, not wanting to attract any attention. I spent the next three days at her place, my limbs were stiff and hurting. I went to see my mother after a fortnight of having left her. I had learnt to adopt a posture which would not reveal the loss of my breasts easily. Passing undetected through a hug required more skills and some quick smooth talking. I got through it by spending most of the time remaining to myself in my room.

Sameer (erstwhile Sumer) called to invite me to go out as men and I set out into the world as a male for the first time! I wore a *thobe* (ankle-length robe worn by men) on which I wore my burka and left home with a unisex bag, informing my mother that I would be returning late. The burka went into the bag before I left the lift and I stepped out onto the street as a man! The world seemed different, the perspective changed, each step I took on the street seemed to take me away from bondage, into a brighter world.

With very few people using the local-city public transport, the facility remained underdeveloped catering to labourers and factory workers. Entering and exiting these buses required skills which can never be acquired by people used to the luxury of commuting in saloon cars. We decided to hop on into one and enjoyed the experience of hanging on the railings when the bus sped as if it was going downhill with its break not functioning. We were looking at each other our jaws clenched and noticed that everyone else on the bus was going around with their business. It didn't take us time to realise that what seemed like a rollercoaster ride was the everyday life of a man. We got off the bus and were quick to learn that we need to run forward to break the inertia. We found ourselves in front of a Mcdonald's outlet. "Let's have burgers," said Sameer. Hardly had we entered the door when we saw the store assistant charging at us as if we had committed a crime! "This is the ladies' entrance," he yelled. We both had a look on our faces which seemed to enquire 'so what?', I was about to ask him what his problem was and then we realised with happiness that it was not the store assistant to blame!

It was the start of a new life, we both were starting our lives yet again, all over from the beginning, and we were not expected to make mistakes as kids are allowed to do. We had to learn to talk, walk, and make sure that we behave like men and do not enter areas designated for ladies, out of habit. For a month we did only this other than the trips to hospital for check-ups.

# 2014

# 2014

# Seven

The scar across my chest had started to heal, the world started looking more promising and then I got the first phone call from Yemen!

"You better kill yourself or be prepared to be tortured to death," was what I heard before the line went dead.

My instinct was to call the number back, but the line wouldn't connect, there was no dial tone, nor could the ring be heard.

I forced myself to believe that this could be a joke, but there lurked an uneasiness in the corner of my confused head. The voice played back in my ears, the last thing I did before going to bed was to try the number again, but to no avail.

I spent a restless night, waking up to the phone ringing only to realize that it was a dream. I woke up by instinct to offer Fajr prayers and saw a missed call on my phone. I might either have slipped deep into sleep or else the caller would have cut the call as soon as the call was transmitted. My hands shivered when I saw that the call was from Yemen, but not from the same number from which I had received the call earlier. I called back the number, but the results weren't any different from my earlier attempts. I could hear the line trying to transmit and then go cold all of a sudden.

Disturbed as I was, I washed myself and stood facing the *Kabah* to offer prayers. I had just intoned my intention for the Fajr prayers and could hear the phone ring again! My faith is such that I offered the prayer in peace, remained on the prayer mat asking forgiveness for my sins and then reached for the phone. The call was from Yemen, from a third number and my attempt to call back was of no help. I was sitting with the phone in my lap when a text message was delivered. It simply said, "You have sinned, you have gone against the will of the creator, you have brought shame not only to the tribe but to all Muslims. You deserve to die. Do yourself a favour by committing suicide, for death by our hands, if you fail to do so, is going to be painful."

This was something that I had not thought of, I was so immersed in my own self, that my worries had not crossed the border of Saudi Arabia till then. I came to know that the head of the Yafa tribe, the tribe to which I belong, had released a fatwa stating what I have done is wrong and would bring misfortune to the maidens of the tribe, if not avenged!

All I wanted was a bunch of tribesmen with daughters, out to hunt me down, for the fatwa stated that every father who is raising a daughter should make an attempt to stop the evil or be prepared to be stricken by curse from the heavens.

I realized that I had more to worry about than waste my emotions on what my brother or the people around me had to say. Here were a bunch of people to whom killing was a casual affair, to assassinate someone who they thought had brought disgrace to the tribe would be a matter of honour to them and might even have their status elevated within the ranks of the tribe for having achieved such noble a feat!

In the month of February, I received a phone call from a friend's husband offering me a job. I agreed to work in the institute where they were offering *Quran* classes on a part-time basis for five hours in the evening. The job involved maintaining the fees and attendance register apart from some administrative work, which took less than a couple of hours for me to complete.

Work was easy, but I did not enjoy the environment as the manager of the institute tried to enforce religion on me. I have always been particular about offering prayers in time and did not really apricate anyone having to tell me stuff. I continued to work as I needed the income to take care of my hormone treatment. Getting a doctor to do the treatment seemed like an impossible task as I didn't have legal documentation. I did not even have my residence permit, without which a trip to the neighbourhood grocery becomes a difficult task. Amna stepped in to help and arranged for a doctor to check me and prescribe the required hormones. Following tests worth $1000, the doctor prescribed Nebido injection to be taken once every three months, the injections were $200 each. The other cheaper option was one that had to be taken once every two weeks but would cost only $10. I went for the cheaper option. The injections made me sweat, anxiety shot up and played havoc with my emotions. I could feel myself being torn apart mentally and physically. These new hormones were working against the Premarin tablets that I had consumed for a very long time.

Somewhere around this point in time, I bought my first car!

I found used cars sold cheaper in Qatar. I asked my cousin there to help me buy a car and send it to Saudi. To my surprise, he sent me money and asked me to buy myself a good car in Saudi itself. My joy knew no bonds, not because he had sent the money but because I realised that I had a family to support me. I got myself a three-year-old Ford Taurus. This car helped me a lot, including retaining my job as my manager would frequently borrow the car to run his personal errands. The car stayed with me for over five years.

Equipped with the car, I used my mornings to visit government offices to try and get my documentation done. Not knowing how and where to start, I tried getting my birth certificate changed. I ran the risk of getting arrested as I did not have my passport or my residence permit. All the documents I had were issued from the hospital and none of these was recognised by any passport or residency agencies. I went to the Yemen embassy to try to get a new passport issued but to no avail. None of the people I met would understand the situation, if at all they did, they had no clue of how to help me. They would all ask me to return with my sponsor. I was ready to live without documents but would not seek help from my brother who was my sponsor.

It was time for my second surgery in the series of three surgeries I was scheduled to undergo. I was not very keen on this surgery as it was meant to salvage whatever they could of my sex organs to try and improve my quality of life. I made sure that the surgery would not be very intrusive, and that the attempts would not be desperate. I was not sold on the idea of relating sex organs to life quality. Not because I was naïve, but because I had gone through much more to be foolish! The surgery was quite painful. I had told no one other than Sameer about the surgery, not even my sisters. Nothing much was achieved from the surgery other than being forced to remain in bed for a week.

The third surgery was just to sew up the ear piercing, and it was just a few hours job.

There was a construction company close to where I worked, and I came to know that the office administrator was planning to leave for Germany to marry his fiancé there. I applied and was offered the job. I started working there. I loved the work and the office. Over four hundred employees worked there, and the office had computers and copiers which I fell in love with. I did not even take the mid-day break and stayed back to help the HR and organise the office.

I had taken the employment as a part-time job but was offered full-time work if I was able to return to work in the evening. I did not think twice before leaving my evening job at the institute and taking up a full-time job at my new place. I started involving myself in sales and became quite good at closing deals. I started handling heavy equipment renting too. With the new rules requiring all salaries to be transferred through the bank online, my services became even more important. I could fit in anywhere and could relieve anyone in any of the divisions. I became quite popular in the company.

Towards the last quarter of the year, I was moved to the sales division with additional responsibility of getting one of the business partner's residence furnished. I was entrusted with a credit card and asked to get the furnishing done. The opportunity gave me the break I was looking for. I could call the shots and I did not shy off from taking decisions. I would walk into furniture showrooms and finalise deals worth hundreds of thousands within a matter of hours. Not only did I love the experience, but I got connected with the right people. I could feel that I am learning fast.

With the government's move to digitize most commercial affairs, my skills on the computer became more valuable. I was able to handle the transition very smoothly. I kept working hard and my work brought excellent results.

Nebido injections were sold at $100 in Egypt and there were enough employees of the company travelling to and from Egypt every month. This served my purpose very well, I changed from the fortnightly dose to Nebido, which was administered once in three months.

The HR head of the company used to visit the passport office every day, I knew that if someone could help me with my documentation, it was him. I told him my story and asked him for help. He happened to have a friend in the Yemen embassy who could help me get a new passport based on a copy of the old passport that I possessed, provided I could produce a certification from the Saudi Health Ministry that I have undergone sex transformation surgery and am now a male. At the outset, this looked like an impossible task. The hospital where I was treated had given me a discharge certificate, but this seemed to have no value. No document other than what the ministry issues was recognised by any other government body.

Approaching the Saudi Health Ministry, or any other ministry for that matter is a tiresome affair for an expatriate, trying to do so without a residence permit is close to impossible, and for someone like me, the chances were minimal. As a female, I would require having my sponsor with me, until certified a male by the ministry, I would remain a female! With my discharge certificate from the hospital and a prayer on my lips, I approached the ministry, I was at the gates even before the cleaners could arrive. Call it luck or my confidence that no one stopped me, and I was able to present my case. I was sent from one table to another, and I could see the confusion on everyone's face, some among them were frustrated too. Towards the end of the day, I was asked to return after a week to be probed by a panel of doctors. I spent the week in fear and anticipation. I tried not to let negativity enter my thoughts but was helpless of arresting the malicious possibilities my mind could cook up. Sleeping became difficult, merciless dreams seemed poised to strike the moment sleep-laden eyes closed in tiredness. My attempts of calming down my overreactive mind didn't seem to help. I somehow survived through the week and reported to the ministry on the scheduled day, at daybreak, to face the panel of doctors. I was prepared to be scanned, x-rayed and inspected. They made me wait in a conference room with a big table and two dozen chairs. A doctor stepped into the room with my file, I expected at least a dozen more to follow, but none did! He scrutinised my file, looked at me and said, "You are not only a man, but you are also a gentleman!" He signed my file and asked me to collect the certificate on my way out.

I couldn't help but pinch myself to make sure that I was not dreaming. I collected the document and very next week received my new passport. The passport opened doors for new possibilities. It took me three months of time and six months of my salary, but I managed to get my sponsorship moved from my brother to my mother and then to the company I was working for.

I had come a long way from where I had started, my brother would not be able to do anything to stop me. Every new day made me more confident, set me free, and made me realize that I had fought a war very few could think of.

*2016*

*Eight*

In the month of January, I obtained my residence permit and within a week got my driving licence.

I had regained my identity!

I wanted to marry!

Even before I had my documents, the thought of marrying would run through my mind often. I was not even sure of obtaining my documents but had faith in God Almighty to bind together two people who loved each other so unconditionally.

She had been with me during the toughest period of my life, composed, patient and never complaining. She materialised whenever I felt that I was slipping down the tunnel, she would somehow appear! She was there beside me to lead me out of the darkest phase of my life. I knew that no force in the world could separate us, I also knew that my lover belonged to the Yafa tribe, a tribe which is known to shoot first and then ask questions.

Nothing other than our love for each other could give me the courage to ask Amna's family for her hand in marriage!

My uncle, his three sons and my cousins in Qatar stood by us. Amna's family agreed to the marriage, and we got married on the 4th of May.

Amna and I had planned a small reception keeping in mind the funds I had available, but we saw everyone coming forward to spice up the wedding. My sisters furnished a room each in the house I had rented, my cousins from Qatar sent gifts in cash and kind, and my uncle and his children helped too. I remember buying furniture worth $3,000 for the bedroom, when I was making the payment my cousin from Riyadh stopped me and paid with his credit card instead. "That's my gift," he said. I carried the furniture by myself, set it up and slept worn out in my new house at the end of the day. Setting up the house meant a lot to me, having a place of my own, a place where I would look after my wife, provide for her, call the shots, where no one else would decide for me. It was a great feeling, a feeling of achievement, of having relatives to help and assist, of not having to face the world alone.

The initial plans of inviting only close family members within the family kept changing until we had more than a hundred women from both families invited.

After a well-attended marriage reception, I drove my wife home in a convoy of cars arranged by my friends, to a new life where I would never be alone.

And I have never been alone, we lead a happy life.

We both work, I continue to work at the same place, the whole office reports to me, and my wife works at a school as she has always done.

I have my bunch of friends; she has her friends and we both have some common friends. Friends from my 'past life' as I wish to classify. I have moved ahead and never felt alone with Amna alongside me all the time. The challenges I face today seem minuscule compared to what I used to fend in my previous life.

Sameer and I look out for someone who might need help, we go all out to provide whatever help and guidance we can, when we find one. We know what it is to be confused, so confused that it gets difficult to breathe. We have seen how grateful they have been when we were able to shine some light into their dark lives, nothing other than seeing the relief on their face has managed to pay back for what we have gone through. While I navigate through the rest of my life, I will remain committed to helping anyone who requires help.

***********

I am not sure how my story is going to end!

I do not belong to the country where I was born, where I was declared and named a girl at birth, where, as they raised me as a girl I nursed and nurtured the boy in me, where they medically aided my body to transform into a female but the male in me refused to accept the fair skin, the soft hands, nimble bones! Where I wept into the dark nights trying to control my emotions triggered by the hormones that were administered, where I treaded on the very thin line between sanity and utter chaos every minute of my life, where I fought my battles when there was a war going in within me between what nature wanted and the drugs that were administered to work against nature having its way.

Mother nature has shown us instances of her wrath and fury when someone obstructs her path when she picks her course. Civilizations have perished, waves have washed towns away, rains have flooded valleys, claiming back yards for every inch mankind has encroached into. Nature lets us be, allows some quick wins too, lets mankind exercise some supremacy over other living beings, as every parent does with their offspring when they are little, and then she disciplines the whole universe with her iron fist, bringing those who feigned might to their knees, begging for mercy. These nudges are not limited to blocking her path, but to her might when mankind gets foolish enough and starts exhibiting courage of ignorance.

Somewhere, unknown to me, without my consent, I was used to attract nature's rage. She hit, but realized that her target was helpless and was armed only with prayers! Not only did she show mercy, but she also breathed courage into me, whispered into my ears to hold on and when she witnessed my determination she conspired with the universe to see me across, to the other side!

All the major events in my life have been triggered by a phone call!

I received one the other day too. The call came from the United Nations office, and they asked me to appear for an interview along with my wife in their Riyadh office. I spent a whole day with them, they were quite intrigued by my story, I could answer most of their queries and for the very few for which I didn't have an answer, I responded with a confident smile.

They are compassionate to my cause and are trying to help me out by finding me a place to migrate to, to settle down and live in peace, what remains of my life. I can't thank them enough, irrespective of what the outcome might be, I have never worried about the days to come, the events of my life have trained me to live the hour!

"Do you know that the Yafa tribesmen are still on the hunt for you?" asks the UN executive with concern in her voice.

"I do," I replied, "I know that the Yafa tribe back in my country continues to see me as an outcast, someone who could bring the hunter charm if hunted down. I realize that it is not a very comfortable situation to be in, but then, life has never been a bed of roses, it was not meant to be nor will it ever be!"

# Notes

# Notes

# Notes